150 Ways to Get Your Zen On

Book 1 – Finding Your Happy Place

SHEILA BURKE

Om Sweet Om Publishing

Printed and bound in the United States

Cover design by Sheila M. Burke © 2013
Photo on last page (kids Zen) © 2013 Carmen Schmid and Lexi Schmid
All other photographs © Sheila M. Burke

ISBN-13: 978-0615794907 (Om Sweet Om)

ISBN-10: 0615794904
Library of Congress Card Number – Pending
150 Ways to Get Your Zen On/ Book 1 – Finding Your Happy Place / Sheila M. Burke
ISBN 0615794904
1st Edition

www.ZenSationalLiving.com

INTRODUCTION

It's the simple things we do or enjoy daily that help us find our Zen. Belly laughs, the warmth of a sunrise, kindness, puppy kisses, or thick, fuzzy socks. The little things that help you to relax and let all the stress slide off your shoulders. This book provides 150 examples of simple thinking designed to help you find your happy place.

Zen is not about never feeling sad, angry, joyful, or having fun; Zen is the understanding that by not clinging (or attaching) ourselves to these feelings, we can free ourselves from them and enjoy life to the fullest.

150 Ways to Get Your 'Zen On

150. Big lazy old doggies
149. Acoustic tunes from *Fistful of Mercy*
148. A hot mug of chai tea with vanilla
147. A blanket fresh out of the dryer
146. Afternoon naps

145. The sound of silence under the night sky

144. *The rhythm of my breath while meditating*

143. Falling in love all over again

142. Thick chunky sweaters

141. Rain on a sunny day

140. A burst of colorful blooms

139. Belly laughs with friends

138. The soft tops of warm muffins

137. Happy endings

136. The smell of new babies

135. Laughing at stupid jokes
134. Seeing shapes in the clouds
133. A good nights sleep
132. Happy tears
131. A Facebook "poke" from a friend

125. **The hum of hummingbirds**

124. *The colors of an Autumn sunset*

123. Tiny little umbrellas on fruity drinks

122. **Laughter from little babies**

121. *Walking on the beach at sunrise*

115. Lying down in a field of wildflowers
114. The smell of lavender upon your fingers
113. Holding hands while skipping
112. Playing Hopscotch
111. Relaxing on a park bench

95. Greeting the sunrise
94. A view that goes on forever
93. The melody of a breeze
92. **An echo**
91. Moments of serendipity

90. **Looking through old photo albums**

89. Freshly baked bread & a warm bowl of soup

88. *Waking up to the peace and quiet of a soft rain*

87. The comforting flicker of a scented candle

86. Connecting with old friends

85. Bonfires and S'Mores
84. Laughing til your cheekbones hurt
83. Being one with nature
82. Seeing the amazement in the eyes of a child
81. Genuine friendships

80. Sweet memories
79. Embracing under a sunset sky
78. STILLNESS
77. Tingling at the thought of someone
76. WAKING UP WITH A SMILE AFTER A GOOD DREAM

75. The smell of campfires
74. Finding $5 in your jeans pocket
73. New socks!
72. Watching someone you love live out a dream
71. Sleeping in

70. Planning a get-away
69. Blades of soft grass tickling your toes
68. Smiling for no reason
67. Fresh applie pie
66. Listening to the rolling waves

65. The thought of springtime after a long hard winter

64. WITNESSING A RANDOM ACT OF KINDNESS

63. Wiggling your toes in the sand

62. the smell of fresh pillowcases

61. The first blooms of the season

60. Kicking and crunching through piles of fallen leaves

59. SPREADING SMILES

58. The first drops of rain on cement

57. GIVING HOPE TO SOMEONE WHO HAS LOST THEIRS

56. Discovering new friends

55. Watching puppies dream

54. **Warm maple syrup on a stack of fluffy pancakes**

53. Sitting quietly with nature

52. Finding your muse

51. Completing a project

50. Moonbeams gently kissing waves
49. The smell and feel of a good book
48. The moment when you realize "I've got this!"
47. **Giggling with a child**
46. A long restful sleep

45. The sweet smell of roses

44. Giggles with girlfriends

43. Catching snowflakes on your tongue

42. GREAT CONVERSATION

41. Feeling at peace

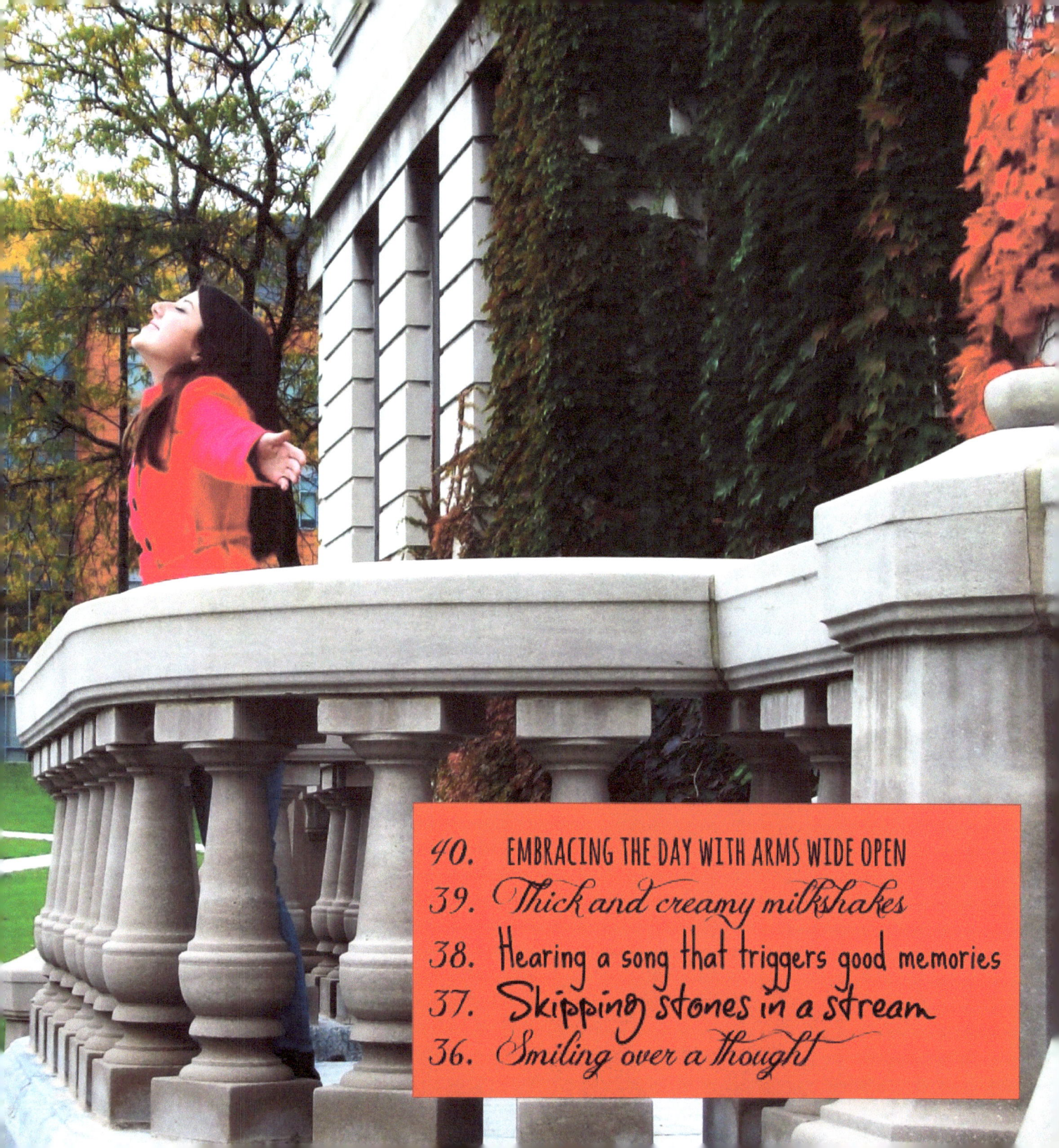

40. EMBRACING THE DAY WITH ARMS WIDE OPEN

39. Thick and creamy milkshakes

38. Hearing a song that triggers good memories

37. Skipping stones in a stream

36. Smiling over a thought

35. Gazing up at the moon and knowing someone you love far away is doing the same

34. TAKING TIME FOR YOURSELF

33. *Realizing you are just as special to someone who you consider special to you*

32. *Trees swaying in a thunderstorm*

31. Watching a rainbow until it fades

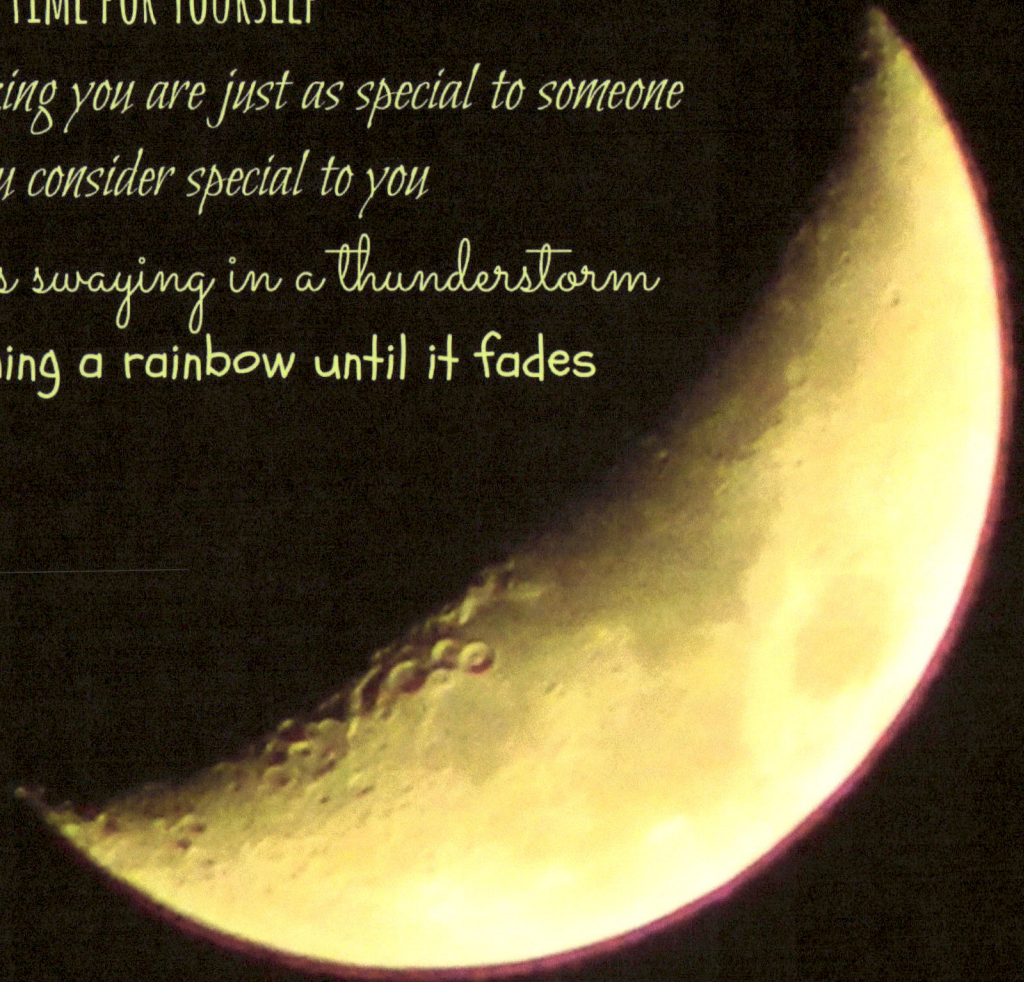

30. An embrace that ripples throughout your entire being

29. **Bacon!**

28. Toasting marshmallows

27. Viewing a sunset from above the clouds

26. Curling up in front of a fire

25. Getting a card in the mail
24. HOMEMADE CHICKEN NOODLE SOUP WHEN YOU'RE SICK
23. Fresh Flowers
22. Walking on the beach under a full moon
21. Waking up to the sound of the ocean

15. The smell of shampoo on freshly washed hair
14. Receiving a handwritten letter
13. The time between wake and sleep
12. CHARTING A NEW COURSE
11. Silk on your bare skin

10. Walking barefoot in the grass

9. Watching the sunshine tickle the ocean waves

8. A warm breeze on a cool afternoon

7. Doing absolutely nothing at all when you should be

6. A FAMILIAR SONG ON A LONG DRIVE

5. Resolving a misunderstanding
4. THE WARMTH OF A SOUL CONNECTION
3. A friend who protects your heart
2. Eating trail mix while cloud watching
1. The chatter of a chipmonk on a still day

ABOUT THE AUTHOR

Sheila Burke is a married mom of three beautiful and strong young adults. Always a dabbler in putting pen to paper, Burke finally started publishing her books in 2010 with the release of her first book Zen-Sational Living. Her journey of self discovery started after getting over the hurdle of raising teenagers without losing *all* of her marbles. Learning how to live a life where stress takes a backseat and love rides shotgun is reflected in her writing. Although she freely admits to losing her Zen now and then, this inspirational author is pleased to share her life's journey with her readers, and has done so in the many titles she has released over the years, on her blog, and through social media. Burke has also designed journals to aid those in recording their own journey.

Books by Sheila Burke:

Zen-Sational Living: A Simple Guide to Finding Your True Self and Maintaining Balance
Booyah! Spirit: 52 Ingredients For A Healthy Soul. Suffering Is Optional
Circle of Soul: at the end, we begin again
Whispers of The Soul
150 Ways to Get Your Zen On: Book 1- Finding Your Happy Place

Blank Journals Designed by Sheila Burke:

Reflections: A Line A Day. My Five Year Journal
Milestones & Memories: A Mother's Journey: Her Five Year Journal
Milestones & Memories: A Father's Journey: His Five Year Journal

www.ZensationalLiving.com
facebook.com/BeZensational

12. When we walk in the rain

11. When my dad and uncle dress up and play tea party with me

10. When I cuddle up with my daddy and fall asleep

~ Mags, age 5

Through the eyes of a child: 12 Ways to Get Your Zen On

9. The smell of bacon
8. Swirly slides at the park
7. Seeing a rainbow outside
6. The smell of popcorn
5. Seeing my mom when she gets home
4. Getting into pajamas right out of the dryer

~ Lexi, age 8

3. Being happy makes me happy... and pancakes
2. Puppies licking my face
1. My daddys laugh

~ Kandi, age 3

www.ingramcontent.com/pod-product-compliance
Lightning Source LLC
Chambersburg PA
CBHW042102040426

42448CB00002B/113